STARTERS
ACTIVITIES

Collecting
Things

Macdonald Educational

About Starters Activities

These books cover a variety of activities for children at school or at home. The projects with their step-by-step illustrations, require the minimum of help from teachers or parents. Most of the words in the text will be in the reading vocabulary of the majority of young readers. Word and sentence length have also been carefully controlled. Extra information and more complex activities are included at the end of each book. Where possible, the child is free to invent and experiment on his own, but concise instructions are given wherever necessary. Teachers and experts have been consulted on the content and accuracy of these books.

Illustrated by: Beverlie Manson

Managing Editor: Su Swallow

Editor: Jennifer Vaughan   **Production:** Stephen Pawley, Rosemary Bishop

Reading consultant: Donald Moyle, author of *The Teaching of Reading* and senior lecturer in education at Edge Hill College of Education

Chairman, teacher advisory panel: F. F. Blackwell, director of the primary extension programme, National Council for Educational Technology

Teacher panel: Stephanie Connell, Sally Chaplin

Colour reproduction by:
Colourcraftsmen Limited

© Macdonald and Company
(Publishers) Limited 1973

0 356 04650 8

Printed by Adams Bros. & Shardlow Ltd., Leicester
Binding by Purnell & Sons Ltd., Paulton. Somerset

Filmsetting by:
Layton-Sun Limited

**First published in 1973 by
Macdonald and Company
(Publishers) Limited
St Giles House
49-50 Poland Street
London W1**

Contents

Colours   pages 1—4
Shapes   pages 5—8
Feel   pages 9—12

Smells   pages 13—15
A beach collection   pages 16—18
A winter collection   pages 19—21

This book is about things
you can collect.

Colours

Here are some red things and
some blue things.

Can you collect some more?

2

Make a picture from the things
you have collected.
Stick them to a piece of paper.

toffee
paper

You can make a coloured window.
Stick toffee papers to cellophane.
Collect as many colours as you can.

4

Shapes

Look for things with odd shapes.
Find sticks, bits of wood
and stones.

This piece of wood looks like a fish.
Try making it more like a fish.
Make other things from wood.

6

Here is a collection of bottles.
Sort out your bottles.
Put the tall ones together.
Put the odd shapes together.

bottle

cloth

glue

ping pong
ball

Use these things to make
bottle people.

8

sugar
lumps

Feel

Find things which have corners.
Collect rough things and smooth things.
Try getting hard things
and soft things.

9

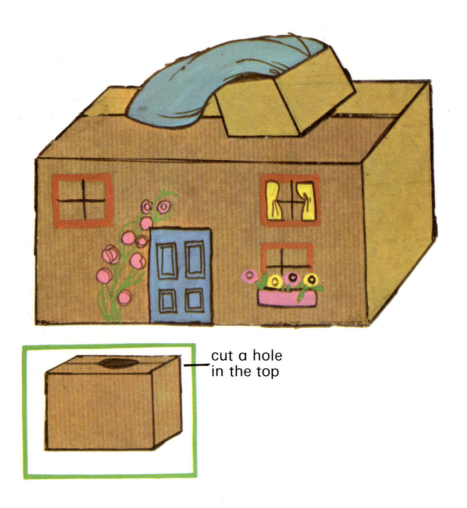

cut a hole
in the top

This is a 'feely' box.
Try making one.
Use a big box. Close it up.
Make a hole in the top of box.
10

cotton wool

mug

tin

buttons

beads

leather things

boxes

Now decorate your 'feely' box.
Put some things in the box.
Here are some things
you might put in it.

11

Stick a piece of an old sock in the hole.

Now ask your friend to put his hand
in the box.
Can he guess what is in it?

12

oranges

nutmeg

cheese

cloves

Smells

Here are some foods with different smells.
Ask your friend to close his eyes.
Can he guess what the foods are?

13

lavender bag

soap

pomander

herbs

dried petals

Long ago, people collected herbs
and flowers to make rooms smell nice.

14

dried
petals

doll stuffed
with herbs

orange stuck
with cloves

herbs

Try collecting some herbs and petals.
You can use them to make presents.

A beach collection

The beach is a good place
for collecting things.

16

Arrange your beach collection
on a net.

Make a collection of coloured pebbles.
Put them under water
to make the colours brighter.
18

A winter collection
Here are some dry plants
collected in winter.

silver paint

Use coloured paints and silver paint
to make the plants look bright.
Decorate your room
with the dry plants.

20

dry plants —

feathers

Show the collection of plants
with other things.
Use feathers, fir cones, and bark.
Make a garden in a box lid.

21

Collecting things words

red
(page 2)

bottles
(page 7)

blue
(page 2)

lemon
(page 8)

toffee
paper
(page 4)

ping pong
ball
(page 8)

sticks
(page 5)

'feely' box
(page 10)

stones
(page 5)

soap
(page 14)

dried petals
(page 14)

silver paint
(page 20)

seaweed
(page 17)

bark
(page 21)

shells
(page 17)

feathers
(page 21)

dry plants
(page 19)

fir cone
(page 21)

23

About collecting

Many people like to collect
things. Some people
like to collect stamps.

Other people collect postcards.

Some birds and animals
collect things.
The bower bird collects
coloured stones.
He decorates the bower he
makes with the stones.

Wood mice collect nuts and
store them for the winter.

Some harder projects

Screws

Make a collection of screws, bolts and nails. See how many different sizes and shapes you can find. You could sew them on to a piece of cloth and pin it to the wall. Make pictures and patterns this way.

Jewels

You could also make a collection of buttons and beads. They will look nice if you set them out on a piece of velvet. If you collect glass buttons and beads you could pretend they are jewels. Find out which jewel each button or bead looks like and then make a label for it.

Stone monsters

Make a collection of stones of strange shapes and colours. Paint faces on these to make monsters. A collection of these will make a monster zoo. If you varnish stones the colours will show up more brightly.

Pressing flowers

Pressing flowers is easy. You can buy special flower presses, but all you really need is a big heavy book, and some blotting paper.

Choose some flowers and leaves you think are pretty. Small flowers are best. Something like a rose is too big to press. Primroses, buttercups and pansies are good for pressing.

Pick the flowers carefully so that you do not damage them. Now open up your book and put a piece of blotting paper on one of the middle pages. Put the flower on top of the blotting paper and then another piece of blotting paper on top of the flower. Close the book, and put some other heavy books on top of it. Do not look at your flower again for at least three weeks. After that you can open up the book and take the flower out. You might like to stick your pressed flowers in an album. You can use them for making pictures.